Graceful Parenting

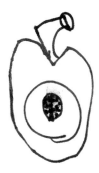

Graceful Parenting

Simple Advice for Raising a Gentle and Loving Child

Eve M. Dreyfus, M.D.

Illustrations by Noah

Celestial Arts
Berkeley • Toronto

A Kirsty Melville Book

Celestial Arts
P.O. Box 7123
Berkeley, California 94707
www.tenspeed.com

Distributed in Australia by Simon and Schuster Australia, in Canada
by Ten Speed Press Canada, in New Zealand by Southern Publishers Group,
in South Africa by Real Books, in Southeast Asia by Berkeley Books,
and in the United Kingdom and Europe by Airlift Book Company.

Cover and interior design by Jennifer Barry Design, Sausalito, CA
Layout production by Kristen Wurz

Library of Congress Cataloging-in-Publication Data
Dreyfus, Eve.
Graceful parenting : simple advice for raising a gentle and
loving child / Eve Dreyfus ; illustrations by Noah.
p.   cm.
"A Kirsty Melville Book."
ISBN 1-58761-132-5
1. Parent and child. 2. Parenting. 3. Child rearing.
4. Child psychology. I. Title.
HQ755.85 .D77 2002
649'.1--dc21
2001008121

First printing, 2002

Printed in Singapore

1 2 3 4 5 6 7 8 9 10 — 05 04 03 02 01

RANCHO CORDOVA

This book is dedicated to Jim Lennon,
my parents, Donald and Sylvie Dreyfus, and
to my brother, Joshua Dreyfus.

Thank you to Jim Lennon, for production
on the initial draft of the manuscript.

&

A special thank you to Robert Scinta,
Noah's father, for helping me raise
such a wonderful child.

Contents

Introduction

This small book will help you raise a happy, healthy, and gentle child.

To make these simple concepts work, start using them from the time

your child is born, but know that you can start any time at any age.

This book is easy to read, but hard to live by.

It will take all the self-control and energy you have.

You will make mistakes sometimes, but if you use these twenty-five

ideas most of the time, this book will work.

The most important thing to remember as a parent is that children

do not purposely misbehave. They are not trying to hurt you or make

your life hard. They are doing the best they can.

Yelling Doesn't Work

You don't need to yell to get your point across. Don't yell at your children and

don't yell in front of your children. Don't yell at their brothers and sisters, and don't yell at

your husband, wife, relatives, or friends. Children copy what they see around them.

If you don't yell and people around them don't yell, your children will learn not to yell.

If you feel like yelling, stop for a moment to get control of yourself.

If you need to leave to do this, excuse yourself from any children present before you yell.

Yelling is contagious. Once it starts, it gets worse.

Remember Not to Expect Too Much of Your Children

Parents often get frustrated or angry with their children because they

expect them to do things they can't do yet. Some parents expect children to act like grown-ups,

but they're not. Don't expect too much from your child. Instead, learn

what to expect from your child at each age by reading a book or talking to a professional.

Children are loud, impolite, selfish, and demanding. This is normal behavior for them.

Don't expect your child to be naturally caring and polite; you have to teach them these behaviors.

No child is born knowing how to act like an adult.

Praise Your Child

Praise your child as often as you can.

Children aren't born knowing they are good at anything.

It is your job to let them know they can be good at everything

they do. If you repeatedly tell them when they're doing well,

they'll believe you and continue to do well.

There is no such thing as too much praise.

Teach Your Child about Emotions

From the time your child is born, talk about how they are feeling.

Teach your children how it feels to be happy, sad, afraid, angry, or nervous.

In simple language, discuss the details of what causes these emotions.

When children understand and talk about their emotions,

they won't get frustrated or angry so easily.

Try Not to Be Critical

Neither children nor grown-ups like to be criticized.

When you criticize a child repeatedly, they begin to feel worthless and unimportant.

Don't criticize a child unless they are in an unsafe situation

and need to learn how to be safe. If you need to criticize, do it gently

and explain the safety issue you are concerned about.

Don't Hit

As with yelling, if children see people

hitting others or being violent, they copy this behavior.

Children who are hit will treat others the same way.

If you feel yourself wanting to hit or physically hurt your child or

someone else in the family, control yourself and don't do it.

If you can't control yourself, then immediately leave the situation.

You may need to seek help from a professional

to stop yourself from being violent.

Don't Argue

Don't argue with your child or the people around you unless

it's about a matter of sickness, safety, or death.

As with yelling, hitting, and violence, children copy arguing.

If you don't argue and are flexible with your children,

they will be flexible too.

Apologize When You're Wrong

Apologize to your child when you do or say the wrong thing.

Many parents think they're weak if they apologize or

admit to a child when they're wrong. This isn't true. If you apologize

when you're wrong, a child will learn to take responsibility

for his or her own wrongdoings too. This is one of the many ways

to develop respect between a parent and a child.

Teach Empathy

Empathy is defined as experiencing the feelings and

thoughts of another person and is a very important part of human relationships.

Empathetic parents raise empathetic children. Teach your child to

understand the ways others feel and think about things. Do this by considering

concrete problems between your child and another person.

Have your child imagine out loud how he or she would feel

and act if he or she were that other person. A child who learns empathy

will easily relate to and understand the world.

Encourage Independence

Children naturally strive toward independence. They actively seek out

activities that they can learn to do themselves. Listen to and support

their independent drives. If you try to do everything for your child, he or she will

become dependent on you and other adults to do things for him

or her unnecessarily. If you nurture a child's drive to become self-sufficient,

you will raise a strong, happy, and independent child.

Turn Around Awkward Moments with Humor and Fun

When you and your child have a difficult moment,

use your sense of humor to turn the moment around. Find a way

to accept the awkwardness and make it fun. Your child

will learn to do the same with his or her difficult moments in life.

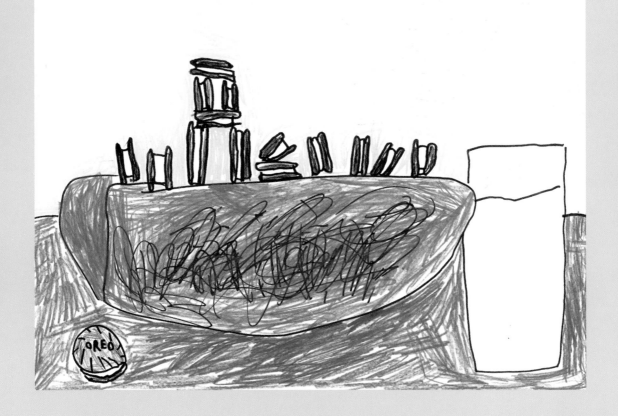

Make Your Child's Schedule More Important Than Your Own

Children do not understand your schedule. Don't get angry if

your child interferes with or interrupts your daily activities.

They do not purposely try to upset your routine. It is up to you to

coordinate your schedule with the needs of your child.

Have Fun

So many parents and children these days are extremely busy.

However, if parents and children don't have fun and

enjoy themselves sometimes, their moods will be negatively affected.

Bad moods can cause yelling, hitting, and arguments.

Take at least two hours a day to play and have fun

with your children. If you have to change your schedule

or skip a regular activity, that's okay.

If You Don't Like Yourself, Your Family, or Other People, Seek Help

Before you have children, it is important to learn to like yourself most

of the time and to get along with people in general. You cannot be a good parent if you do

not have good relationships with others. If you have bad feelings about yourself,

are angry at your parents and family, or cannot get along with others—get help.

People who tend to have poor relationships raise children who also have

poor relationships. If you seek help, you can break this cycle.

No Guns

Don't give children access to guns.

If you do own guns, don't ever show your children where they are.

Letting guns fall into the hands of a child often leads

to terrible accidents and deaths.

Try Not to Push Too Much

Many children have demanding schedules from a young age.

They do many hours of homework and have multiple extracurricular activities.

Don't push your child so much that they are always under pressure.

Pressure can cause a child to rebel or to have poor self-confidence.

NS

Practice Giving Your Child the Control

Children and parents often argue and fight because they both want to be in control

of a situation. When a child is struggling for control, as often as possible,

hand over the control. The more often a child is able to take charge of and control

his or her life, the less rebellious he or she will be in the long run.

Listen

From birth, children tell or show you

what they need and want. If you, as a parent, are able to place

your own desires, concerns, and expectations aside,

you will be better able to understand what your children need.

Children frequently know what they need more accurately

than the adults who care for them.

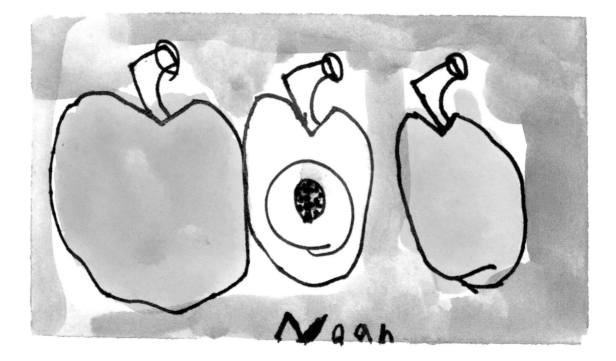

Be Available

Being available means listening to your child's problems—

when he or she has been bullied or has failed at something—and helping

your child to independently solve his or her problems.

This means refraining from instructing your child to always do things your way.

Listening to your child's failures without telling him or her exactly

what to do will boost your child's self-confidence.

Be Affectionate

Tell and show your child how much you love him or her.

Touch and hold your child a lot. Physical touch and affection is very

important for a child's development. If you show your child a

great deal of affection, he or she will become secure knowing how

you feel and will treat others affectionately.

Expose Your Child to Many Activities

Children should be exposed to as many forms of art, music, science, literature, and

physical activities as possible. Constantly explain and talk about activities

while you are engaging in them. A child's mind is fluid and easily absorbs all input.

The more activities children are exposed to, the better they will be able

to process the world around them.

Give All the Time; Don't Withhold

Give your child the attention and time that he or she needs as often as possible.

Don't be withholding. Children crave your attention, and they want

to feel special in your eyes. They have large holes inside of them that need to be filled.

Children who do not receive enough attention to fill these holes feel deprived.

Such feelings of deprivation lead to poor self-confidence and self-blame.

If you give your child your attention and time, they will feel special

and will stop craving attention.

Don't Expose Your Child to Sexuality

Sexuality and pride in one's body are important parts of life; however, young children should not be exposed to excessive adult sexuality and nudity. Children who view nudity or adult sexuality can become preoccupied with early sexual feelings and can be traumatized by this. It is very important to separate children from adult sexuality while simultaneously promoting pride in their own bodies.

POMEgranate NS

Try to Avoid Time-Outs

If a child misbehaves, always try to reason with him or her

in order to avoid a time-out. The use of time-outs is frequently misunderstood

by children, who can feel very hurt when given a time-out

or can turn the punishment into further opportunity to misbehave.

Children understand simple explanations of behavior.

Simply explaining the wrongdoing to the child is a much more effective

and direct way to manage negative behaviors.

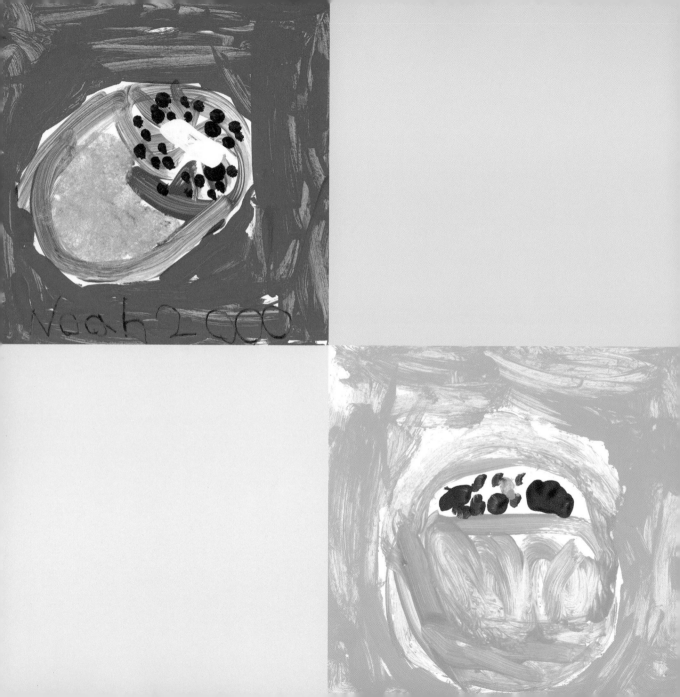

Give Your Child As Many Choices in Life As Possible

Adults frequently try to control children's decisions. When a child

is stifled by controlling adults, he or she may rebel and

become oppositional. Give choices rather than orders. The more choices

a child has, the less likely he or she will become rebellious.

Noah

In Conclusion

I hope these approaches will help

parents raise happy, confident, and independent children.

In addition, these concepts can be applied to

all interpersonal relationships to help achieve strong and

fulfilling human bonds that will last a lifetime.

About the Author

Dr. Eve Dreyfus is a board certified child psychiatrist who has treated thousands of behaviorally disturbed children and their families for over ten years. She obtained a Bachelor of Science degree in Psychology from Brown University. She went on to obtain a doctorate of medicine from Boston University. She completed a one-year internship in internal medicine and went on to complete four years of adult and child psychiatry training at the University of California in San Diego. She has made over 150 media appearances and currently resides in California.

About the Artist

Noah is the seven-year-old son of Dr. Eve Dreyfus. He currently attends a Montessori school and enjoys art, soccer, playing the piano, and swimming. Noah loves animals and talks about being a scientist.